ONE MEETS HIS DESTINY OFTEN
ON THE ROAD HE TAKES TO AVOID IT.
- Jean de La Fontaine

- PROVERB
YOU CANNOT BE LOST ON A
ROAD THAT IS STRAIGHT.

ALL PEOPLE SMILE IN THE SAME LANGUAGE.
- Unknown

"THE PATH IS MADE BY WALKING."
- Antonio Machado

- PROVERB
"A BAD WORKER BLAMES HIS TOOLS."

"TIME NEVER GETS TIRED OF RUNNING."
- Egyptian Proverb

"KNOW YOURSELF... AND YOU SHALT KNOW THE GODS."
- EGYPTIAN PROVERB

"THERE IS NO SHAME IN NOT KNOWING; THE SHAME LIES IN NOT FINDING OUT."
- RUSSIAN PROVERB

"FALL SEVEN TIMES,
STAND UP EIGHT."
- JAPANESE PROVERB

"TURN YOUR FACE TOWARD THE SUN AND THE SHADOWS FALL BEHIND YOU."
- MAORI PROVERB

"SOME PEOPLE GO THROUGH A FOREST
AND SEE NO FIREWOOD." - ENGLISH PROVERB

"BEGIN TO WEAVE AND GOD WILL GIVE THE THREAD." - GERMAN PROVERB

"THOSE WHO WISH TO SING ALWAYS FIND A SONG." | - SWEDISH PROVERB

"A MOTHER UNDERSTANDS WHAT A CHILD DOES NOT SAY." — YIDDISH PROVERB

"IF YOU CAN WALK YOU CAN DANCE.
IF YOU CAN TALK YOU CAN SING."
- ZIMBABWE PROVERB

"CHEESE, WINE, AND FRIENDS MUST BE OLD TO BE GOOD." - CUBAN PROVERB

"EVEN FROM A FOE A MAN MAY LEARN WISDOM."
- GREEK PROVERB

"IF YOU DON'T HAVE TIME TO DO IT RIGHT
YOU MUST HAVE TIME TO DO IT OVER."
- RUSSIAN PROVERB

"IF YOU WANT TO BE RESPECTED,
YOU MUST RESPECT YOURSELF."
- SPANISH PROVERB

THANK YOU.
THE END.

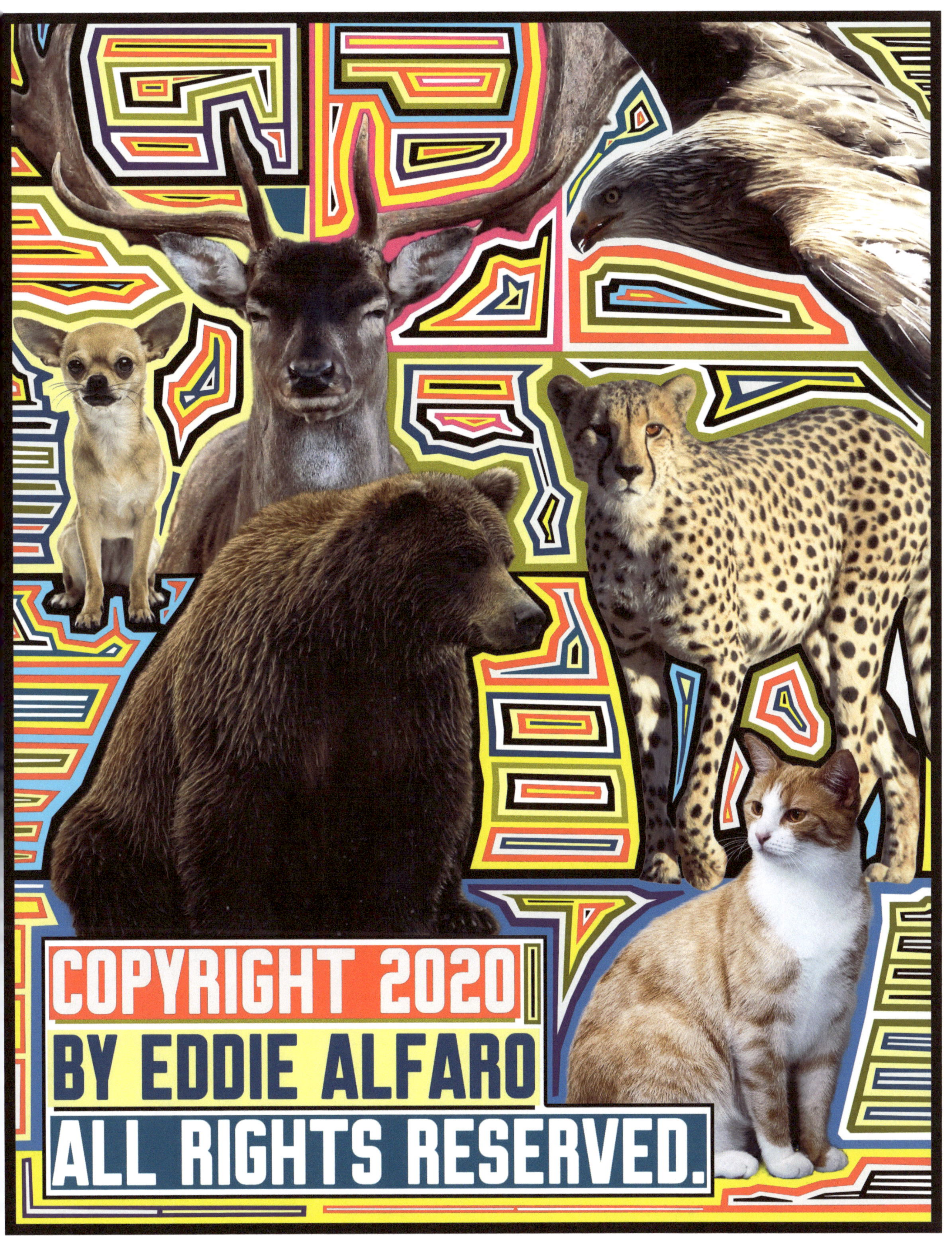
COPYRIGHT 2020
BY EDDIE ALFARO
ALL RIGHTS RESERVED.

MORE BOOKS AT:

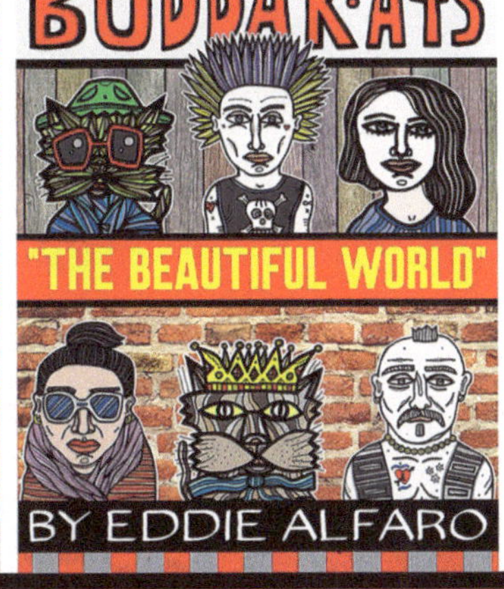

631ART.COM